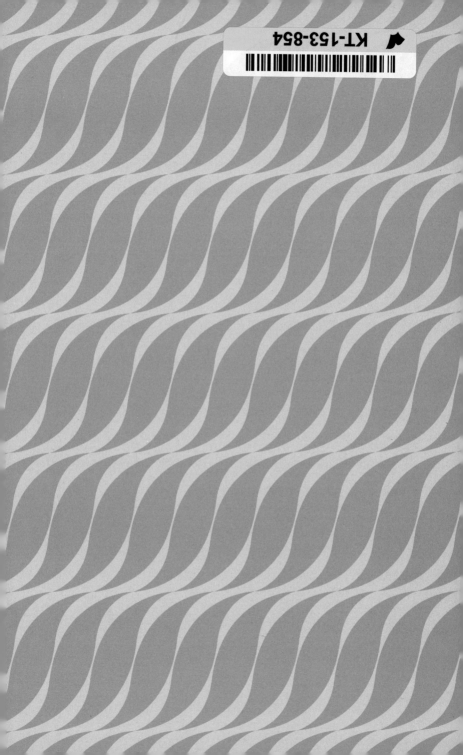

KT-153-854

BEST-EVER
BURGERS

Consultant Editor:
Valerie Ferguson

southwater

Contents

Introduction

Hamburgers – named after Hamburg steak, a term for minced beef – have conquered the world as everyone's favourite snack. Yet there is a huge difference between the patties in fast food outlets and the succulent home-made variety. Real burgers are filling, nourishing and totally delicious. They are also a true culinary experience – this book is packed with flavoursome recipes based on chicken, fish, lamb, nuts and pulses, as well as the original beef. Extra flavourings, such as cheese, herbs, chillies and dried fruit, are incorporated, and many recipes include delicious sauces and relishes. The clear instructions and step-by-step illustrations virtually guarantee success.

Most of these recipes work well whether you choose to cook them on a barbecue, to use a conventional grill or to shallow fry. Mini-burgers are delicious deep fried. From salmon to bean, from Tex-Mex to teriyaki, there is no denying the endless versatility of the burger.

Techniques

Mincing Meat

Minced meats of all kinds are easily obtainable, but when you want to use a particular well-trimmed cut, you can mince it yourself.

1 Trim the meat well and cut it into 4 cm/1½ in cubes or strips, then feed it through a mincing machine.

2 If you are using a food processor, trim the meat carefully and cut it into cubes. Place in the machine fitted with the metal blade, and pulse.

3 In between times, stir the meat around so that it is evenly minced. Do not overprocess to a purée or your burgers will be tough.

4 You can also mince meat by hand. First trim the meat well. Using a large chef's knife, cut the meat into cubes, then chop into smaller and smaller cubes. Continue chopping until you have the consistency you want.

Barbecuing

Burgers and barbecues are a classic combination. Do not start cooking until the flames have died down and the coals are glowing red, but covered with a thin layer of ash. An adjustable grill is the easiest way of altering the heat; otherwise take advantage of the fact that the edges of the barbecue are likely to be less hot than the centre.

Brush the grill bars with oil before adding the burgers. Timings vary depending on the thickness of the burger, its main ingredient, the type and size of the barbecue and even the weather. The times shown are for guidance only and you should always check that the burgers are cooked through before serving.

Grilling

Always preheat the grill and brush the grill rack with oil. Brush the burgers with oil or a sauce before cooking. Timings are similar to barbecues, but vary depending on the type of grill.

1 Place the burgers about 8 cm/3 in away from the heat, turn once during cooking and brush with oil or the sauce again.

Frying

Fish burgers and some veggie burgers have a delicate texture that makes them unsuitable for barbecues and grilling. These are best shallow fried and, of course, other types of burgers may be fried too. Heat a heavy-based frying pan and add about 1 cm/½ in vegetable oil. When it is hot, carefully add the burger using a fish slice and fry over a moderate heat. Turn once during cooking and when golden and cooked through, remove with a fish slice and drain on kitchen paper.

Occasionally, a recipe calls for deep frying. Heat plenty of oil in a deep-fat fryer to 190°C/375°F or until a cube of bread browns in 30 seconds. Carefully lower the burgers into the oil and cook for the time given in the recipe. Remove and drain on kitchen paper. Do not overcrowd the pan; cook in batches if necessary.

Timing Guide for Barbecuing Burgers (2 cm/³⁄₄ in thick)

Type of burger	Heat	Total cooking time
Bean	hot	8–10 minutes
Beef	hot	6–8 minutes
Chicken	medium	8–12 minutes
Fish	medium	8–10 minutes
Lamb	medium	10–15 minutes

Basic Recipes

A Basic Burger

Home-made burgers are simple to make and extremely versatile.

Makes 4

INGREDIENTS
115 g/4 oz minced beef or other meat
5 ml/1 tsp mixed dried or chopped
   fresh herbs
salt and freshly ground black pepper

1 Place the minced beef or other meat in a bowl and thoroughly break it up with a fork. Add the dried or fresh herbs and season well with salt and pepper. Mix together well.

2 Bring the mixture together with your hands and form into four burgers. Cook on a moderately hot barbecue or under a preheated grill for about 8 minutes, turning once.

These relishes are very easy and quick to prepare and will liven up a wide variety of burgers.

Quick Barbecue Relish

45 ml/3 tbsp sweet pickle
15 ml/1 tbsp Worcestershire sauce
30 ml/2 tbsp tomato ketchup
10 ml/2 tsp prepared mustard
15 ml/1 tbsp cider vinegar
30 ml/2 tbsp brown sauce

1 Mix together the pickle, Worcestershire sauce, tomato ketchup and prepared mustard.

2 Add the vinegar and brown sauce and mix well. Cover and chill and use when required.

COOK'S TIP: Barbecue and tomato relishes can be used immediately, but will also keep for a few days in the fridge.

Tomato Relish

15 ml/1 tbsp olive oil
1 onion, finely chopped
1 garlic clove, crushed
25 g/1 oz/2 tbsp flour
30 ml/2 tbsp tomato ketchup
300 ml/½ pint/1¼ cups passata
5 ml/1 tsp sugar
15 ml/1 tbsp chopped fresh parsley

1 Heat the oil in a pan. Add the onion and garlic and fry for 5 minutes, stirring occasionally. Add the flour and cook for 1 minute more, stirring the mixture continuously.

2 Stir in the tomato ketchup, passata, sugar and fresh parsley. Bring to the boil and cook for 10 minutes, stirring frequently. Cover the relish and chill until required.

VARIATION: For a hot and spicy version of this relish, add 10 ml/ 2 tsp chilli sauce and 1 green chilli, finely chopped, at step 2.

Cucumber Relish

½ cucumber
2 celery sticks, chopped
1 green pepper, seeded and chopped
1 garlic clove, crushed
300 ml/½ pint/1¼ cups natural yogurt
15 ml/1 tbsp chopped fresh coriander
freshly ground black pepper

1 Dice the cucumber and place in a large bowl. Add the celery, green pepper and crushed garlic.

2 Stir in the yogurt and fresh coriander. Season with the pepper. Cover and chill. Use the same day.

Herby Fish Burgers with Lemon & Chive Sauce

The wonderful flavour of fresh herbs and the citrus sauce makes these fish burgers the catch of the day.

Serves 4

INGREDIENTS
350 g/12 oz potatoes, peeled
75 ml/5 tbsp milk
350 g/12 oz haddock or
    hoki fillets, skinned
15 ml/1 tbsp lemon juice
15 ml/1 tbsp creamed
    horseradish sauce
30 ml/2 tbsp chopped fresh parsley
flour, for dusting
115 g/4 oz/2 cups fresh
    wholemeal breadcrumbs
salt and freshly ground black pepper
flat leaf parsley sprigs, to garnish
mangetouts and a sliced tomato and
    onion salad, to serve

FOR THE LEMON & CHIVE SAUCE
thinly pared rind and juice of
    ½ small lemon
120 ml/4 fl oz/½ cup dry
    white wine
2 thin slices fresh root ginger
10 ml/2 tsp cornflour
30 ml/2 tbsp snipped fresh chives

1 Place the potatoes in a large saucepan of water and boil them for 15–20 minutes. Drain and mash with the milk and season to taste with salt and pepper.

2 Process the fish, together with the lemon juice and horseradish sauce, in a blender or food processor to a purée. Mix together with the potatoes and parsley. Preheat the grill.

3 With floured hands, shape the mixture into eight burgers and coat with the breadcrumbs. Chill in the fridge for 30 minutes.

4 To make the sauce, cut the lemon rind into julienne strips and put into a saucepan, together with the lemon juice, wine, ginger and seasoning.

5 Simmer, uncovered, for 6 minutes. Blend the cornflour with 15 ml/1 tbsp cold water. Add to the saucepan and simmer until clear.

6 Cook the burgers under a moderate grill for 5 minutes on each side, until they are browned.

7 Stir the chives into the sauce immediately before serving. Serve the sauce hot with the burgers, garnished with sprigs of flat leaf parsley and accompanied by mangetouts and a sliced tomato and onion salad.

11

Smoked Fish Burgers

These delicious burgers are very easy to prepare and can be made with inexpensive offcuts of any good-quality smoked fish.

Serves 4

INGREDIENTS
450 g/1 lb cooked, mashed potatoes
450 g/1 lb cooked mixed white
   and smoked fish such as haddock
   or cod, flaked
25 g/1 oz/2 tbsp butter, diced
45 ml/3 tbsp chopped
   fresh parsley
1 egg, separated
plain flour, for shaping
1 egg, beaten
about 50 g/2 oz/1 cup
   fine breadcrumbs made with
   stale bread
vegetable oil, for frying
freshly ground black pepper
crisp salad, to serve

2 Divide the fish and potato mixture into eight equal portions, then, with floured hands, form each portion into a flat burger.

3 Beat the remaining egg white with the whole egg. Carefully dip each fish burger in the beaten egg, then in the fine breadcrumbs.

COOK'S TIP: If using smoked cod or haddock, try to use naturally smoked fish rather than the brightly dyed variety. For extra-special burgers, use smoked trout or salmon.

VARIATIONS: If preferred, substitute fresh dill for the parsley used here. You might also like to serve these burgers with a little soured cream.

1 Place the potatoes in a bowl and beat in the fish, butter, parsley and egg yolk. Season the mixture to taste with freshly ground black pepper.

4 Heat the oil in a frying pan, then shallow fry the fish burgers for about 3–5 minutes on each side, until they are crisp and golden brown. Drain on kitchen paper and serve hot with a crisp salad.

Maryland Burgers with Tartare Sauce

Made from fresh crab meat and served with a delicious sauce, these American seafood burgers are a gourmet treat.

Serves 4

INGREDIENTS
1 egg, beaten
30 ml/2 tbsp mayonnaise
15 ml/1 tbsp Worcestershire sauce
15 ml/1 tbsp sherry
30 ml/2 tbsp finely chopped fresh parsley
30 ml/2 tbsp finely chopped fresh
   chives or dill
675 g/1½ lb fresh crab meat
45 ml/3 tbsp vegetable oil
salt and freshly ground black pepper
salad leaves, lemon slices and fresh chives,
   to garnish

FOR THE SAUCE
1 egg yolk
15 ml/1 tbsp white wine vinegar
30 ml/2 tbsp Dijon mustard
250 ml/8 fl oz/1 cup vegetable oil
30 ml/2 tbsp lemon juice
60 ml/4 tbsp finely chopped
   spring onions
30 ml/2 tbsp chopped, drained capers
60 ml/4 tbsp finely chopped gherkins
60 ml/4 tbsp finely chopped
   fresh parsley

1 Mix together the egg, mayonnaise, Worcestershire sauce, sherry and herbs. Season with salt and pepper. Gently fold in the crab meat.

2 Divide into eight portions and form into oval burgers. Place on a baking sheet between layers of greaseproof paper and chill for at least 1 hour.

3 Meanwhile, make the sauce. Beat the egg yolk with a wire whisk until smooth. Add the vinegar and mustard and season to taste, whisking for about 10 seconds to blend. Whisk in the oil in a slow, steady stream.

4 Add the remaining ingredients and mix well. Check the seasoning. Cover and chill. Preheat the grill.

5 Brush the burgers with the oil. Place on an oiled baking sheet in one layer. Grill under a medium heat for about 5 minutes on each side, until they are golden brown. Serve hot with the tartare sauce, garnished with salad leaves, lemon slices and chives.

Crispy Cod Burgers

A crisp, golden breadcrumb crust conceals a melt-in-the-mouth, ultra-smooth fish filling within.

Serves 4

INGREDIENTS
300 g/11 oz cod fillet
1 large mild onion, one-third sliced,
    the rest finely chopped
45 ml/3 tbsp mayonnaise
400 g/14 oz potatoes, boiled, peeled,
    coarsely mashed and cooled
plain flour, for shaping
1 egg, beaten
200 g/7 oz/3½ cups fresh
    white breadcrumbs
oil, for deep frying
salt and freshly ground
    white pepper
sprigs of fresh parsley,
    to garnish

1 Lay the cod fillet on a large heatproof plate and sprinkle with sliced onion. Season with salt and pepper. Cover with foil and stand the plate over a saucepan of simmering water. Cook for 15 minutes, or until the fish is opaque and flakes easily. Allow to cool.

VARIATION: These burgers would also work well made with other types of white fish, such as haddock, whiting or coley.

2 Mix together the chopped onion, mayonnaise, a pinch of salt and white pepper and the potatoes.

3 Discard the sliced onion and the skin and bones from the fish. Put the fish in a plastic bag and pound it with a rolling pin until it is finely flaked.

4 Mix the cod into the potatoes. With floured hands, shape the mixture into eight oval, flat burgers. Press and mould the mixture firmly to press out any air as you shape the burgers. Dip the burgers in the beaten egg and coat them in the fresh white breadcrumbs. Chill for 30 minutes.

5 Heat the oil to 180°C/350°F. Fry the burgers in pairs to prevent them from bursting. Turn them in the oil, allowing about 3 minutes on each side, until they are crisp and golden. Drain well on kitchen paper.

6 Place two cod burgers on each plate. Garnish each serving with fresh parsley sprigs and serve immediately.

Highland Burgers

Scotland's most famous fish is used in these sophisticated salmon burgers, served with spicy mayonnaise.

Serves 4

INGREDIENTS
350 g/12 oz potatoes
350 g/12 oz salmon fillet, skinned
   and finely chopped
30–45 ml/2–3 tbsp chopped
   fresh dill
15 ml/1 tbsp lemon juice
flour, for coating
45 ml/3 tbsp vegetable oil
salt and freshly ground
   black pepper
mixed salad leaves, to serve

FOR THE SPICY MAYONNAISE
350 ml/12 fl oz/1½ cups mayonnaise
15 ml/1 tbsp Dijon mustard
5 ml/1 tsp Worcestershire sauce
dash of Tabasco sauce

1 First, make the spicy mayonnaise. Mix together the mayonnaise and the Dijon mustard, then stir in the Worcestershire sauce and Tabasco sauce to taste. Cover the dish and chill in the fridge until required.

2 Put the potatoes, unpeeled, in a saucepan of boiling salted water and parboil them for 15 minutes. Drain and leave until cool enough to handle, then peel.

3 Meanwhile, combine the salmon, dill and lemon juice in a large bowl and season to taste with salt and freshly ground black pepper.

4 Shred the potatoes into strips on the coarse side of a grater. Add to the salmon mixture and mix gently with your fingers, breaking up the strips of potato as little as possible.

5 Divide the salmon and potato mixture into eight portions. Shape each into a burger, pressing well together. Flatten the burgers to about 1 cm/½ in thickness. Coat the salmon burgers lightly in flour, shaking off the excess.

6 Heat the oil in a large frying pan. Add the burgers and fry, turning once, for 5 minutes, or until crisp and golden brown all over. Drain on kitchen paper and serve with the spicy mayonnaise and mixed salad leaves.

COOK'S TIP: The potatoes will be sticky – it is their starch that helps hold the cakes together. If necessary, you can dampen your hands a little when shaping the cakes, but do not let the cakes become too wet.

Fish Mini-burgers, Thai-style

Small in size and big on flavour, these spicy little burgers, served with cucumber relish, pack a real punch.

Makes about 12

INGREDIENTS
300 g/11 oz white fish fillet,
    such as cod, cut into chunks
30 ml/2 tbsp ready-made
    red curry paste
1 egg
30 ml/2 tbsp Thai fish sauce
5 ml/1 tsp sugar
30 ml/2 tbsp cornflour
3 kaffir lime leaves, shredded
15 ml/1 tbsp chopped fresh coriander
50 g/2 oz green beans, finely sliced
oil, for frying
Chinese mustard cress, to garnish

FOR THE CUCUMBER RELISH
60 ml/4 tbsp Thai coconut or
    rice vinegar
60 ml/4 tbsp water
50 g/2 oz sugar
1 head pickled garlic, chopped
1 cucumber, quartered and sliced
4 shallots, finely sliced
15 ml/1 tbsp finely chopped fresh
    root ginger
2 red chillies, chopped

1 To make the cucumber relish, bring the vinegar, water and sugar to the boil. Stir until the sugar dissolves, then remove from the heat and cool.

2 Combine the rest of the relish ingredients together in a bowl and pour over the vinegar mixture.

3 Combine the fish, curry paste and egg in a food processor and process well. Transfer the mixture to a bowl, add the rest of the ingredients, except for the oil and garnish, and mix well.

4 Mould and shape the mixture into burgers about 5 cm/2 in in diameter and 5 mm/¼ in thick.

5 Heat the oil in a wok or deep-fat fryer. Fry the mini-burgers, a few at a time, for about 4–5 minutes, or until they are golden. Remove and drain on kitchen paper. Garnish with Chinese mustard cress and serve with the cucumber relish.

Teriyaki Chicken Burgers

These neat and attractive Japanese-style burgers, glazed with a tasty teriyaki sauce, take only minutes to prepare.

Serves 4

INGREDIENTS
400 g/14 oz minced chicken
1 small egg
60 ml/4 tbsp grated onion
7.5 ml/1½ tsp sugar
7.5 ml/1½ tsp Japanese
    soy sauce (shoyu)
cornflour, for coating
½ bunch spring onions, white parts only,
    finely shredded, to garnish
15 ml/1 tbsp oil

FOR THE TERIYAKI SAUCE
30 ml/2 tbsp sake or dry
    white wine
30 ml/2 tbsp sugar
30 ml/2 tbsp mirin
    (Japanese rice wine)
30 ml/2 tbsp Japanese soy
    sauce (shoyu)

COOK'S TIP: For the barbecue or grill, use the mixture to make smaller chicken burgers and brush them frequently with the teriyaki sauce as they are cooking.

1 Mix the minced chicken with the egg, onion, sugar and soy sauce until the ingredients are thoroughly combined and well bound together. This will take about 3 minutes, and the mixture will be quite sticky, which gives a good texture.

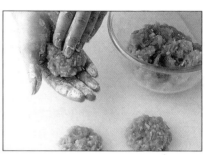

2 Shape the mixture into 12 small, flat round burgers and dust them lightly all over with cornflour.

3 Soak the shredded spring onions in a bowl of ice-cold water for 5 minutes and drain thoroughly.

4 Heat the oil in a frying pan. Place the chicken burgers in the pan in a single layer and cook over a moderate heat for 3 minutes. Turn the burgers over and cook for a further 3 minutes on the second side.

5 Mix the ingredients for the sauce and pour it into the pan. Turn the burgers occasionally until they are evenly glazed. Move or gently shake the pan constantly to prevent the sauce from burning.

6 Arrange the chicken burgers on a warm serving plate and top with the shredded spring onions. Serve the burgers immediately.

Lamb Burgers with Cucumber Sauce

Lightly spiced and flavoured with dried fruits and pine nuts, these burgers are the perfect choice for a summer barbecue.

Serves 4

INGREDIENTS
675 g/1½ lb lean minced lamb
1 small onion, finely chopped
8 dried apricot halves, finely chopped
60 ml/4 tbsp pine nuts
25 g/1 oz/⅓ cup fine dry breadcrumbs
10 ml/2 tsp mild curry powder
1 egg
salt and freshly ground black pepper
4 pitta breads, heated and cut in half, and mixed green salad, to serve

FOR THE CUCUMBER SAUCE
½ cucumber, peeled and grated
300 ml/½ pint/1¼ cups natural yogurt
30 ml/2 tbsp chopped fresh mint

1 Combine the lamb, onion, apricots, pine nuts, breadcrumbs, curry powder, egg, salt and pepper in a bowl. Mix well together with your fingers until thoroughly blended.

2 Divide the mixture into eight portions and shape each portion into a small, flat burger. Cover and chill in the fridge for 30 minutes.

3 Meanwhile, for the sauce, squeeze the grated cucumber in a double thickness of kitchen paper to extract excess water. Mix together the cucumber, natural yogurt and fresh mint. Season to taste with salt and freshly ground black pepper. Preheat the grill or prepare a charcoal fire.

4 Grill or barbecue the burgers until they are cooked to your taste (about 10 minutes for medium). Turn them halfway through cooking to ensure that they brown and cook evenly.

5 Serve the lamb burgers in the warmed pitta halves, accompanied by the mixed green salad and the cucumber sauce.

Lamb Burgers with Cucumber Relish

Tangy cucumber relish perfectly complements these spicy lamb burgers.

Serves 4

INGREDIENTS
675 g/1½ lb lean minced lamb
1 medium onion, finely chopped
15 ml/1 tbsp paprika
30 ml/2 tbsp chopped fresh parsley
30 ml/2 tbsp chopped fresh mint
salt and freshly ground black pepper
4 burger buns, split open, to serve

FOR THE CUCUMBER RELISH
1 large cucumber, thinly sliced
1 small red onion, thinly sliced
45 ml/3 tbsp lime or lemon juice
30 ml/2 tbsp vegetable oil
60 ml/4 tbsp chopped fresh mint
2 spring onions, finely chopped

1 To make the relish, combine the ingredients in a large, non-metallic bowl. Cover and chill for at least 2 hours or overnight.

2 In a bowl, combine the lamb, onion, paprika, parsley, mint and a little salt and pepper. Mix thoroughly. Preheat the grill.

3 Divide the lamb mixture into four equal portions and shape each into a burger 2.5 cm/1 in thick. Grill, allowing 5 minutes on each side for medium and 8 minutes on each side for well-done. Toast the cut surfaces of the buns briefly. Serve the burgers in the buns, with the cucumber relish.

Lamb Burgers with Melting Centres

You can prepare these surprise burgers in advance and freeze them between sheets of greaseproof paper.

Makes 6

INGREDIENTS
450 g/1 lb minced lamb
dash of Worcestershire sauce
pinch of dried marjoram
50 g/2 oz Bel Paese, Feta or other tasty, but
    not strong cheese, diced
olive oil, for brushing
salt and freshly ground black pepper
mixed salad and black olives, to serve

1 Place the minced lamb in a bowl with the Worcestershire sauce, marjoram, and salt and pepper to taste and mix thoroughly.

2 Divide the lamb mixture into six and push a little of the diced cheese into the middle of each portion. Mould the lamb mixture around the piece of cheese with dampened hands, shape into burgers, cover and leave to stand for 10–20 minutes. Preheat the grill.

3 Brush the grill pan and the lamb burgers lightly with olive oil and grill them under a high heat, for 3–5 minutes on each side, or until they are cooked to your liking. Serve the lamb burgers with a mixed salad and black olives.

Minty Lamb Burgers with Redcurrant Chutney

These rather special burgers take a little extra time to prepare, but are well worth the effort involved.

Serves 4

INGREDIENTS
500 g/1¼ lb minced lean lamb
1 small onion, finely chopped
30 ml/2 tbsp finely chopped fresh mint
30 ml/2 tbsp finely chopped fresh parsley
115 g/4 oz Mozzarella cheese
oil, for brushing
salt and freshly ground black pepper

FOR THE CHUTNEY
115 g/4 oz/1½ cups fresh or frozen and
  thawed redcurrants
10 ml/2 tsp clear honey
5 ml/1 tsp balsamic vinegar
30 ml/2 tbsp finely chopped fresh mint

2 Cut the Mozzarella into four slices or cubes. Place them on four of the lamb rounds. Top each with another round of meat mixture.

3 Press together firmly, making four flattish burger shapes and sealing in the cheese completely.

4 Place all the ingredients for the chutney in a bowl and mash them together with a fork. Season well with salt and pepper.

1 Mix together the lamb, onion, mint and parsley until evenly combined. Season well with salt and pepper. Divide the mixture into eight equal pieces and use your hands to press them into flat rounds.

5 Brush the burgers with oil and cook them over a moderately hot barbecue for about 15 minutes, turning once, until brown. Serve with the redcurrant chutney.

VARIATION: If redcurrants are not available, serve the burgers with ready-made redcurrant jelly.

Best-ever American Burgers

The Americans have burger making down to a fine art.

Serves 4

INGREDIENTS
15 ml/1 tbsp vegetable oil
1 small onion, finely chopped
450 g/1 lb lean minced beef
1 large garlic clove, crushed
5 ml/1 tsp ground cumin
10 ml/2 tsp ground coriander
30 ml/2 tbsp tomato purée or ketchup
5 ml/1 tsp wholegrain mustard
dash of Worcestershire sauce
30 ml/2 tbsp chopped fresh mixed herbs
    (parsley, thyme and oregano or marjoram)
15 ml/1 tbsp lightly beaten egg
flour, for shaping
oil, for frying (optional)
salt and freshly ground black pepper
4 burger buns, mixed salad, chips
    and relish, to serve

1 Heat the oil in a frying pan, add the onion and cook for 5 minutes, until softened. Remove from the pan, drain on kitchen paper and leave to cool.

2 Mix together the beef, garlic, spices, tomato purée or ketchup, mustard, Worcestershire sauce, herbs, beaten egg and seasoning. Stir in the onions.

3 Sprinkle a board with flour and shape the mixture into four burgers. Cover and chill for 15 minutes.

4 Fry the burgers in a little oil over a medium heat for about 5 minutes each side, according to taste. Alternatively, cook under a medium grill or on a barbecue for the same time. Serve in the buns, with salad, chips and relish.

Herbed Burgers

Bring a touch of Italian sunshine to your table with these delicious burgers.

Serves 4

INGREDIENTS
675 g/1½ lb lean minced beef
1 garlic clove, finely chopped
1 spring onion, very finely chopped
45 ml/3 tbsp chopped fresh basil
30 ml/2 tbsp chopped fresh parsley
40 g/1½ oz/3 tbsp butter
salt and freshly ground black pepper

FOR THE TOMATO SAUCE
45 ml/3 tbsp olive oil
1 medium onion, finely chopped
300 g/11 oz tomatoes, chopped
a few fresh basil leaves
45–60 ml/3–4 tbsp water
5 ml/1 tsp sugar
15 ml/1 tbsp white wine vinegar
sprigs of parsley and basil, to garnish

1 To make the tomato sauce, heat the oil and sauté the onion until translucent. Add the tomatoes and cook for 2–3 minutes. Add the basil, cover, and cook for 7–8 minutes.

2 Add the water, sugar and vinegar, and cook for 2–3 minutes. Season, allow to cool slightly, and pass the sauce through a food mill or strainer.

3 Combine the meat with the garlic, spring onion and herbs. Season and form into four burgers.

4 Fry in melted butter over moderate heat until done on both sides. Place on a serving plate and keep warm. Reheat the sauce. Serve with the burgers, garnished with herbs.

Surf & Turf

Originally made with steak, this interpretation of an American theme will delight the eyes and the palate.

Serves 4

INGREDIENTS
225 g/8 oz lean minced beef
115 g/4 oz/2 cups fresh
   wholemeal breadcrumbs
4 spring onions, sliced
1 garlic clove, crushed
5 ml/1 tsp chilli powder
30 ml/2 tbsp oil
salt and freshly ground
   black pepper
mangetouts, to serve

FOR THE SAUCE
25 g/1 oz/2 tbsp plain flour
150 ml/¼ pint/⅔ cup dry
   white wine
50 ml/2 fl oz/¼ cup vegetable stock
120 ml/4 fl oz/½ cup double cream
115 g/4 oz/½ cup cooked, peeled
   tiger prawns

FOR THE CROUTES
4 slices white bread
25 g/1 oz/2 tbsp butter

1 Mix the minced beef with the breadcrumbs, spring onions, garlic and chilli powder. Season well and form into four equal rounds.

2 Heat the oil in a frying pan and cook the burgers for about 7 minutes, turning them frequently.

3 For the sauce, add the flour to the frying pan and cook for 1 minute. Gradually pour in the wine, stock and cream and add the prawns. Cook, stirring constantly, for 5 minutes.

VARIATION: If tiger prawns are unavailable, this recipe works equally well with smaller prawns or shrimps. Remember to thaw frozen ones thoroughly before using.

4 For the croûtes, stamp out four 10 cm/4 in rounds from the bread. Melt the butter in a large frying pan and add the bread. Cook for 2–3 minutes, turning once. Remove and drain on kitchen paper, then transfer to a serving plate. Place the burgers on top and spoon the sauce over them. Serve with mangetouts.

Beef & Mushroom Burgers

As well as tasting utterly scrumptious, these burgers are a healthy low-fat version with extra fibre.

Serves 4–5

INGREDIENTS
1 small onion, chopped
150 g/5 oz/2 cups small
    cup mushrooms
450 g/1 lb lean minced beef
50 g/2 oz/1 cup fresh
    wholemeal breadcrumbs
5 ml/1 tsp dried mixed herbs
15 ml/1 tbsp tomato purée
flour, for shaping
salt and freshly ground black pepper
Quick Barbecue or Tomato Relish,
    salad, and burger buns or pitta bread,
    to serve

2 Divide the mixture into eight to ten pieces, then press into burger shapes using lightly floured hands.

3 Cook the burgers in a non-stick frying pan or under a hot grill for 12–15 minutes, turning once, until evenly cooked. Serve with relish and salad, in burger buns or pitta bread.

1 Place the onion and mushrooms in a food processor and process until finely chopped. Add the beef, breadcrumbs, herbs, tomato purée and seasonings. Process for a few seconds, until the mixture binds together but still has some texture.

COOK'S TIP: The mixture is quite soft, so handle carefully and use a fish slice for turning to prevent the burgers from breaking up during the cooking process.

Oregon Blue Cheese Burgers

This succulent American-style burger is filled with melting blue cheese and makes a really substantial lunch.

Serves 4

INGREDIENTS
900 g/2 lb lean minced beef
1 garlic clove, crushed
30 ml/2 tbsp chopped
    fresh parsley
30 ml/2 tbsp chopped
    fresh chives
2.5 ml/½ tsp salt
225 g/8 oz Oregon Blue or Danish Blue
    cheese, crumbled
4 burger buns, split and toasted
freshly ground black pepper
tomato slices, lettuce and mustard or
    ketchup, to serve

2 Make a slit in the side of each burger to form a pocket. Fill each pocket with a quarter of the cheese.

3 Close the pockets to seal the cheese inside the patties. Heat a ridged grill pan or preheat the grill.

1 In a bowl, combine the beef, garlic, parsley, chives, salt and a little pepper. Mix lightly together, then form into four thick burgers.

4 Cook the burgers 4–5 minutes on each side for medium-rare, or 6–7 minutes for well-done. Place the burgers in the split buns. Serve immediately, with sliced tomatoes and lettuce leaves, and mustard or ketchup if desired.

Homeburgers

Cheeseburgers with a difference – melted Cheddar
cheese is encased in a burger, subtly flavoured with mango chutney.

Serves 4

INGREDIENTS
450 g/1 lb lean minced beef
2 slices of bread, crusts removed
1 egg
4 spring onions, roughly chopped
1 garlic clove, chopped
15 ml/1 tbsp mango chutney
10 ml/2 tsp dried mixed herbs
50 g/2 oz/⅓ cup Cheddar cheese
salt and freshly ground black pepper
4 burger buns, to serve

1 Put the meat, bread, egg, spring onions and garlic in a food processor. Add a little salt and pepper and process until evenly blended. Add the chutney and herbs and process again.

COOK'S TIP: When grilling the burgers, do not place them too close to the heat or they will burn on the outside before the middle has cooked properly.

2 Divide the burger mixture into four equal portions and pat into flat rounds, with damp hands, to stop the meat from sticking.

3 Cut the cheese into four equal pieces and put one in the centre of each piece of beef. Wrap the meat around the cheese to make a burger. Chill in the fridge for 30 minutes. Preheat the grill.

4 Grill the burgers for 5–8 minutes on each side, then put each burger in a bun and serve immediately with your favourite trimmings.

Tex-Mex Burgers in Tortillas

If you fancy a change from ordinary burgers in baps, try this easy Tex-Mex version. Serve with a crisp green salad.

Serves 4

INGREDIENTS
500 g/1¼ lb lean minced beef
1 small onion, finely chopped
1 small green pepper, seeded and
    finely chopped
1 garlic clove, crushed
oil, for brushing
4 fresh tortillas
salt and freshly ground
    black pepper
chopped fresh coriander, to garnish
mixed salad leaves, to serve

FOR THE GUACAMOLE SAUCE
2 ripe avocados
1 garlic clove, crushed
2 tomatoes, chopped
juice of 1 lime or lemon
½ small green chilli, chopped
30 ml/2 tbsp chopped fresh coriander

1 Mix together the minced beef, onion, pepper and garlic and season well with salt and pepper.

2 Using your hands, shape the mixture into four large, round burgers and brush them with oil.

3 For the guacamole sauce, cut the avocados in half, remove the stones and scoop out the flesh.

4 Mash the avocado flesh roughly and mix in the garlic, tomatoes, lime or lemon juice, chilli and coriander. Season to taste with salt and pepper.

5 Cook the burgers on a medium hot barbecue or under a preheated grill for 8–10 minutes, turning once, until they are brown.

6 When the burgers are almost cooked, heat the tortillas quickly on the barbecue for about 15 seconds each side and then place a spoonful of guacamole and a burger on each. Wrap the tortilla around the filling. Garnish with coriander and serve with mixed salad leaves.

COOK'S TIP: The guacamole sauce should be made not more than about an hour before it's needed, or it will start to brown. If it has to be left to stand, sprinkle a little extra lime or lemon juice over the top and stir it in just before serving.

Spicy Bite-size Burgers

These irresistible coconut-flavoured burgers from Indonesia make a wonderful snack or party dish.

Makes 22

INGREDIENTS
2.5 ml/½ tsp each coriander
    and cumin seeds,
    dry fried
115 g/4 oz freshly grated coconut,
    or desiccated coconut, soaked in
    60–90 ml/4–6 tbsp boiling water
350 g/12 oz finely minced beef
1 garlic clove, crushed
a little beaten egg
15–30 ml/1–2 tbsp
    plain flour
groundnut oil, for frying
salt
thin lemon or lime wedges,
    to serve

1 Place the dry fried coriander and cumin seeds in a mortar and grind thoroughly with a pestle.

2 In a bowl, mix the grated or moistened desiccated coconut with the minced beef.

3 Add the ground spices to the meat and coconut mixture, together with the garlic, salt to taste and sufficient beaten egg to bind.

4 Divide the meat mixture into evenly sized portions, each about the size of a walnut, and form the portions into burger shapes.

5 Dust the burgers with flour. Heat the oil in a frying pan and fry the patties for 4–5 minutes until both sides are golden brown and cooked through. Serve with lemon or lime wedges, to squeeze over.

Mexican Beef Burgers

The only thing missing from this Mexican platter is a glass of tequila.

Serves 4

INGREDIENTS
4 corn cobs
50 g/2 oz/1 cup dry white breadcrumbs
90 ml/6 tbsp milk
1 small onion, finely chopped
5 ml/1 tsp ground cumin
2.5 ml/½ tsp cayenne pepper
2.5 ml/½ tsp celery salt
45 ml/3 tbsp chopped fresh coriander
900 g/2 lb lean minced beef
4 burger buns
60 ml/4 tbsp mayonnaise
4 tomato slices
½ iceberg lettuce or other leaves such as
    frisée or Webb's
salt and freshly ground black pepper
1 large packet corn chips, to serve

1 Bring a large saucepan of water to the boil, then add a pinch of salt and cook the corn cobs for 15 minutes.

2 Combine the breadcrumbs, milk, onion, cumin, cayenne, celery salt and fresh coriander in a large bowl.

3 Add the minced beef to the bowl and mix it in thoroughly, using your hands, until the mixture is evenly blended.

4 Divide the beef mixture into four equal portions. Place the portions between sheets of clear film, or use damp hands, and press down the mixture to form flat burger shapes.

5 Preheat a moderate grill and cook for 10 minutes for medium burgers or 15 minutes for well-done burgers, turning them over once during the cooking time.

6 Split and toast the burger buns, spread with mayonnaise and sandwich the burgers in the buns with the tomato slices, lettuce or other salad leaves and seasoning. Serve the burgers with corn chips and the corn cobs.

Japanese-style Burgers

This recipe makes soft and moist burgers that are delicious with rice, especially with the mooli topping, which adds its own refreshing flavour.

Serves 4

INGREDIENTS
30 ml/2 tbsp oil, plus extra for
    greasing hands
1 small onion, finely chopped
500 g/1¼ lb minced beef
50 g/2 oz/1 cup fresh
    white breadcrumbs
1 egg
5 ml/1 tsp salt
115 g/4 oz shiitake mushrooms,
    stems discarded and caps sliced
200 g/7 oz mooli (daikon radish),
    finely grated and drained in a sieve
4 shiso leaves, finely
    shredded (optional)
30 ml/2 tbsp soy sauce
freshly ground black pepper
boiled rice, to serve

1 Heat 15 ml/1 tbsp of the oil in a frying pan and fry the onion gently until it is soft, but not browned. Leave to cool.

2 Put the minced beef in a large bowl with the fried onion, breadcrumbs and egg. Season with the salt and pepper. Knead well by hand until the ingredients are thoroughly combined and the mixture becomes sticky. It is important to keep the meat soft and juicy for this recipe. Divide the mixture into four.

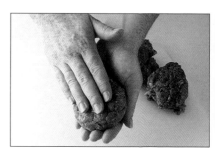

3 Put a little oil on your hands. Take a portion of the mixture and throw it from one hand to the other five or six times to remove any air. Then shape the mixture into a 2 cm/¾ in thick burger. Repeat the process with the remaining mixture.

4 Heat the remaining oil in a frying pan and add the burgers. Fry over a high heat until browned on one side, then turn over. Place the shiitake mushrooms in the pan, next to the burgers, cover and allow to cook over a low heat for 3–4 minutes, or until the burgers are cooked through, stirring the mushrooms occasionally.

5 Top the burgers with the mooli, shiitake mushrooms and shiso leaves (if using). Pour 7.5 ml/1½ tsp soy sauce over each burger just before it is served with the rice.

COOK'S TIP: Shiso is a small herb with a slightly minty taste. If not available, sweet basil or mint may be used instead.

Stilton Burgers

Slightly more up-market than the traditional burger – lightly melted
Stilton cheese is encased in a crunchy burger that is absolutely delicious.

Serves 4

INGREDIENTS
450 g/1 lb minced beef
1 onion, finely chopped
1 celery stick, chopped
5 ml/1 tsp dried mixed herbs
5 ml/1 tsp prepared mustard
50 g/2 oz/½ cup crumbled
    Stilton cheese
4 burger buns
salt and freshly ground
    black pepper
salad and mustard pickle,
    to serve

1 Place the minced beef in a bowl,
together with the onion and celery.
Season well with salt and pepper.

2 Stir in the herbs and mustard,
bringing them together to form a
firm mixture. Divide the mixture into
eight equal portions. Place four on
a chopping board and flatten each
one slightly.

3 Place the crumbled cheese in the
centre of each portion, dividing it
equally among them.

4 Flatten the remaining mixture and
place on top. Mould the mixture
together, encasing the crumbled
cheese, and shape into four burgers.
Preheat the grill.

5 Grill under a medium heat for
10 minutes, turning once, or until
cooked through. Split the buns and
place a burger inside each. Serve with
salad and mustard pickle.

Cheeseburgers with Spicy Avocado Relish

A mouth-watering treat – 100 per cent beef burgers are topped with melting cheese and a creamy avocado relish.

Serves 6

INGREDIENTS
900 g/2 lb lean minced beef
6 slices Gruyère or Cheddar cheese
6 burger buns, split and toasted
2 large tomatoes, sliced
salt and freshly ground black pepper
fresh parsley sprigs, to garnish

FOR THE AVOCADO RELISH
1 large ripe avocado,
   peeled and stoned
1 spring onion, chopped
10 ml/2 tsp lemon juice
5 ml/1 tsp chilli powder
30 ml/2 tbsp chopped fresh tomato

1 Mash the avocado with a fork. Stir in the spring onion, lemon juice, chilli powder and chopped tomato. Set aside.

2 Preheat the grill. Divide the beef into six portions. Shape each portion into a burger 2 cm/¾ in thick and season. Grill the burgers for 5 minutes on each side for medium-rare, 8 minutes on each side for well-done.

3 Top each burger with a slice of cheese and grill for 30 seconds, until melted. Place a burger in each toasted bun. Top with a slice of tomato and a spoonful of avocado relish and serve, garnished with a sprig of parsley.

Russian Hamburgers

Every Russian family has its own version of this homely hamburger. The mixture can also be shaped into small round meatballs.

Serves 4

INGREDIENTS
115 g/4 oz/2 cups fresh white breadcrumbs
45 ml/3 tbsp milk
450 g/1 lb finely minced lean beef
1 egg, beaten
30 ml/2 tbsp plain flour
30 ml/2 tbsp sunflower oil
salt and freshly ground black pepper
tomato sauce, pickled vegetables and
    crispy fried onions, to serve

1 Put the breadcrumbs in a bowl and spoon over the milk. Set aside to soak for 10 minutes.

2 Add the minced beef and beaten egg and season to taste with salt and freshly ground black pepper. Mix all these ingredients together thoroughly.

3 Divide the mixture into four equal portions and shape into oval burgers, each one about 10 cm/4 in long and 5 cm/2 in wide. Coat each burger with the flour.

4 Heat the oil in a frying pan and fry the burgers for about 8 minutes on each side, until browned. Serve with tomato sauce, pickled vegetables and fried onions.

Pizza Burgers

Inspired by Italy's most famous dish, these burgers are topped with tomato, Mozzarella cheese and anchovies.

Serves 6

INGREDIENTS
½ slice white bread, crusts removed
45 ml/3 tbsp milk
675 g/1½ lb minced beef
1 egg, beaten
50 g/2 oz/⅔ cup dry breadcrumbs
vegetable oil, for frying
2 beefsteak or other large
   tomatoes, sliced
15 ml/1 tbsp chopped
   fresh oregano
1 Mozzarella cheese, cut into
   6 slices
6 drained canned anchovies,
   cut in half lengthways
salt and freshly ground
   black pepper

1 Preheat the oven to 200°C/400°F/ Gas 6. Put the bread and milk into a small saucepan and heat very gently until the bread absorbs all the milk. Mash it to a pulp and leave to cool.

2 Put the beef into a bowl with the bread mixture and the egg and season with salt and freshly ground black pepper. Mix well, then shape the mixture into six burgers. Sprinkle the breadcrumbs on to a plate and dredge the burgers, coating them thoroughly.

3 Heat about 5 mm/¼ in oil in a large frying pan. Add the burgers and fry for 2 minutes on each side, until brown. Transfer to a greased ovenproof dish in a single layer.

4 Lay a slice of tomato on top of each burger, sprinkle with oregano and season with salt and pepper. Place the Mozzarella slices on top and sprinkle with pepper. Arrange two strips of anchovy in a cross on top of each slice of Mozzarella.

5 Bake for 10–15 minutes, until the Mozzarella has melted. Serve hot, straight from the dish.

Rockburger Salad with Sesame Croûtons

This dish is a variation on the ingredients that make up the all-American beefburger in a sesame bun.

Serves 4

INGREDIENTS

900 g/2 lb lean minced beef
1 egg
1 medium onion, finely chopped
10 ml/2 tsp French mustard
2.5 ml/½ tsp celery salt
115 g/4 oz Roquefort or other blue cheese
1 large sesame seed loaf
45 ml/3 tbsp olive oil
1 small iceberg lettuce
50 g/2 oz rocket or watercress
175 ml/6 fl oz/¾ cup French dressing
4 ripe tomatoes, quartered
4 large spring onions, sliced
salt and freshly ground black pepper

1 Place the beef, egg, onion, mustard, celery salt and pepper in a mixing bowl. Combine thoroughly. Divide the mixture into 16 portions, each weighing about 50 g/2 oz.

COOK'S TIP: To make the French dressing, put 45 ml/3 tbsp white wine vinegar in a bowl and whisk in salt and pepper to taste. Gradually whisk in 150 ml/¼ pint/⅔ cup extra virgin olive oil. Stir in 5 ml/1 tsp Dijon mustard and 15 ml/1 tbsp chopped fresh herbs.

2 Flatten the pieces between two sheets of clear film or waxed paper to form 13 cm/5 in rounds.

3 Place 15 g/½ oz of the cheese on eight of the burgers. Sandwich with the remainder and press the edges. Store between clear film or waxed paper and chill until ready to cook.

4 To make the sesame croûtons, preheat the grill. Remove the sesame crust from the bread, then cut the crust into short fingers. Moisten with olive oil and toast evenly for 10–15 minutes.

5 Season the burgers to taste with salt and black pepper and grill for about 10 minutes, turning once, until browned and cooked through.

6 Toss the salad leaves with the dressing, then distribute among four large plates. Place two rockburgers in the centre of each plate and the tomatoes, spring onions and sesame croûtons around the edge.

Chick-pea & Coriander Burgers with Tahini

These spicy little burgers are equally good served hot or cold. For a more substantial snack, tuck them into pockets of pitta bread with salad.

Serves 4

INGREDIENTS
2 x 400 g/14 oz cans
    chick-peas, drained
2 garlic cloves, crushed
1 bunch spring onions,
    white parts only, chopped
10 ml/2 tsp ground cumin
10 ml/2 tsp ground coriander
1 fresh green chilli, seeded and
    finely chopped
30 ml/2 tbsp chopped
    fresh coriander
1 small egg, beaten
30 ml/2 tbsp plain flour
seasoned flour, for shaping
oil, for shallow frying
salt and freshly ground
    black pepper
lemon wedges and fresh coriander,
    to garnish

FOR THE TAHINI & LEMON DIP
30 ml/2 tbsp tahini
juice of 1 lemon
2 garlic cloves, crushed

1 Put the chick-peas in a blender or food processor and process until smooth. Add the garlic, spring onions, cumin and ground coriander. Process again until well mixed.

2 Scrape the mixture into a bowl and stir in the chilli, fresh coriander, egg and flour. Mix well and season. If the mixture is very soft add a little more flour. Chill for about 30 minutes.

3 Make the dip. Mix the tahini, lemon juice and garlic in a bowl, adding a little water if the sauce is too thick. Set aside.

4 Using floured hands, shape the chick-pea mixture into 12 burgers. Heat the oil in a frying pan and fry them, in batches, for about 1 minute on each side, until crisp and golden. Drain on kitchen paper and serve with the dip and lemon and coriander garnish.

VARIATION: Another quick and easy sauce is made by mixing Greek yogurt with a little chopped chilli and fresh mint.

Cheese & Potato Burgers

Crisp on the outside and deliciously smooth on the inside, these veggie burgers are the perfect way to use up leftover vegetables.

Serves 4

INGREDIENTS
about 450 g/1 lb/3 cups mashed potato
about 225 g/8 oz cooked cabbage or
    kale, shredded
1 egg, beaten
115 g/4 oz/1 cup grated Cheddar cheese
nutmeg, freshly grated
plain flour, for coating
oil, for frying
salt and freshly ground black pepper
fresh flat leaf parsley, to garnish
grilled mushrooms, to serve

1 Mix the potato, cabbage or kale, egg, cheese, nutmeg and seasoning. Divide and shape into eight burgers.

2 Chill for an hour. Toss the burgers in the flour. Heat about 1 cm/½ in oil in a frying pan until it is quite hot.

3 Carefully slide the burgers into the hot oil and fry on each side for about 3 minutes, until golden and crisp. Drain on kitchen paper and serve with grilled mushrooms and fresh parsley.

Veggie Burgers

Mushrooms, vegetables and nuts are combined in these flavour-packed and low-fat burgers.

Serves 4

INGREDIENTS
115 g/4 oz mushrooms, finely chopped
1 small onion, chopped
1 small courgette, chopped
1 carrot, chopped
25 g/1 oz/¼ cup unsalted peanuts
   or cashews
115 g/4 oz/2 cups
   fresh breadcrumbs
30 ml/2 tbsp chopped
   fresh parsley
5 ml/1 tsp yeast extract
fine oatmeal or flour, for shaping
salt and freshly ground
   black pepper
salad, to serve

1 Dry fry the mushrooms in a non-stick pan, stirring, for 8–10 minutes to drive off all the moisture.

2 Process the onion, courgette, carrot and nuts in a food processor until beginning to bind together.

3 Stir in the mushrooms, breadcrumbs, parsley, yeast extract and seasoning to taste. With the oatmeal or flour, shape into four burgers. Chill.

4 Cook the burgers in a non-stick frying pan with very little oil or under a hot grill for 8–10 minutes, turning once, until cooked and golden brown. Serve hot with a crisp salad.

Aduki Bean Burgers

Although not quick to make, these burgers are a delicious alternative to shop-bought ones, so it is worth making up several batches for the freezer.

Makes 12

INGREDIENTS
200 g/7 oz/1 cup brown rice
1 onion, chopped
2 garlic cloves, crushed
30 ml/2 tbsp sunflower oil
50 g/2 oz/4 tbsp butter
1 small green pepper, seeded and chopped
1 carrot, coarsely grated
400 g/14 oz can aduki beans, drained
    (or 125 g/4½ oz/⅔ cup dried beans,
    soaked and cooked)
1 egg, beaten
115 g/4 oz/1 cup grated mature cheese
5 ml/1 tsp dried thyme
50 g/2 oz/½ cup roasted hazelnuts or
    toasted flaked almonds
wholemeal flour or cornmeal, for coating
oil, for frying
salt and freshly ground black pepper
burger buns, salad and relish,
    to serve

1 Cook the rice according to the instructions, allowing it to overcook slightly so that it is soft. Strain the rice and transfer it to a large bowl.

2 Fry the onion and garlic in the oil and butter, together with the pepper and carrot, for about 10 minutes, until the vegetables are softened.

3 Mix this vegetable mixture into the rice, together with the aduki beans, egg, cheese, thyme, hazelnuts or almonds and plenty of seasoning. Chill until quite firm.

4 Shape into 12 burgers, using wet hands if the mixture sticks. Coat the burgers in wholemeal flour or cornmeal and set aside.

5 Heat 1 cm/½ in oil in a large, shallow frying pan and fry the burgers, in batches, for about 3 minutes on each side, until browned. Pat the burgers dry on kitchen paper and serve in buns with salad and relish.

COOK'S TIP: To freeze the burgers, cool them after cooking, then open freeze them before wrapping and bagging. Use within 6 weeks. Cook from frozen by baking in a preheated moderately hot oven for 20–25 minutes.

Red Bean & Mushroom Burgers

Vegetarians and vegans can enjoy these healthy veggie burgers. With salad and pitta bread they make a substantial meal.

Serves 4

INGREDIENTS

15 ml/1 tbsp olive oil
1 small onion, finely chopped
1 garlic clove, crushed
5 ml/1 tsp ground cumin
5 ml/1 tsp ground coriander
2.5 ml/½ tsp ground turmeric
115 g/4 oz/1½ cups finely
    chopped mushrooms
400 g/14 oz can red kidney beans
30 ml/2 tbsp chopped
    fresh coriander
wholemeal flour, for shaping
olive oil, for brushing
salt and freshly ground black pepper
salad and warmed pitta bread,
    to serve

1 Heat the oil in a large pan and cook the onion and garlic over a moderate heat, stirring, until softened. Add the spices and cook for a further minute, stirring continuously.

2 Add the mushrooms and cook, stirring, until softened and dry. Remove from the heat.

3 Drain and rinse the beans thoroughly and then mash them well with a fork.

4 Stir the beans into the pan, with the fresh coriander, mixing thoroughly. Season well with salt and pepper.

5 Using floured hands, form the mixture into four flat burger shapes. If the mixture is too sticky to handle, mix in a little flour.

6 Brush the burgers with oil and cook on a hot barbecue or under a preheated grill for 8–10 minutes, turning once, until golden brown. Serve with a crisp salad and warmed pitta bread.

This edition is published by Southwater

Southwater is an imprint of
Anness Publishing Ltd
Hermes House
88-89 Blackfriars Road
London SE1 8HA
tel. 020 7401 2077
fax 020 7633 9499

Published in the USA by
Anness Publishing Inc.
27 West 20th Street
Suite 504
New York
NY 10011

Distributed in the UK by
The Manning Partnership
251–253 London Road East
Batheaston
Bath BA1 7RL
tel. 01225 852 727
fax 01225 852 852

Distributed in Australia by
Sandstone Publishing
Unit 1, 360 Norton Street
Leichhardt
New South Wales 2040
tel. 02 9560 7888
fax 02 9560 7488

All rights reserved. No part of this publication may be reproduced, stored in a retrieval system, or transmitted
in any way or by any means, electronic, mechanical, photocopying, recording or otherwise, without the prior
written permission of the copyright holder.

© 2000, 2001, 2002 Anness Publishing Limited

Publisher: Joanna Lorenz
Editor: Valerie Ferguson
Series Designer: Bobbie Colgate Stone
Designer: Andrew Heath
Editorial Reader: Penelope Goodare
Production Controller: Joanna King

Recipes contributed by: Catherine Atkinson, Alex Barker, Carla Capalbo, Lesley Chamberlain, Kit Chan,
Frances Cleary, Trisha Davies, Roz Denny, Joanna Farrow, Christine France, Sarah Gates, Masaki Ko,
Lesley Mackley, Norma MacMillan, Sallie Morris, Jenny Stacey, Hilaire Walden, Laura Washburn,
Steven Wheeler, Judy Williams.

Photography: William Adams-Lingwood, Karl Adamson, Edward Allwright, Steve Baxter, James Duncan,
Ian Garlick, Michelle Garrett, Amanda Heywood, David Jordan, Don Last, Patrick McLeavey, Michael Michaels,
Thomas Odulate, Juliet Piddington.

3 5 7 9 10 8 6 4

Notes:
For all recipes, quantities are given in both metric and imperial measures and, where appropriate,
measures are also given in standard cups and spoons. Follow one set, but not a mixture,
because they are not interchangeable.
Standard spoon and cup measures are level.

1 tsp = 5 ml   1 tbsp = 15 ml

1 cup = 250 ml/8 fl oz

Australian standard tablespoons are 20 ml. Australian readers should use 3 tsp in place of 1 tbsp for
measuring small quantities of gelatine, cornflour, salt, etc.
Medium eggs are used unless otherwise stated.

Printed and bound in China

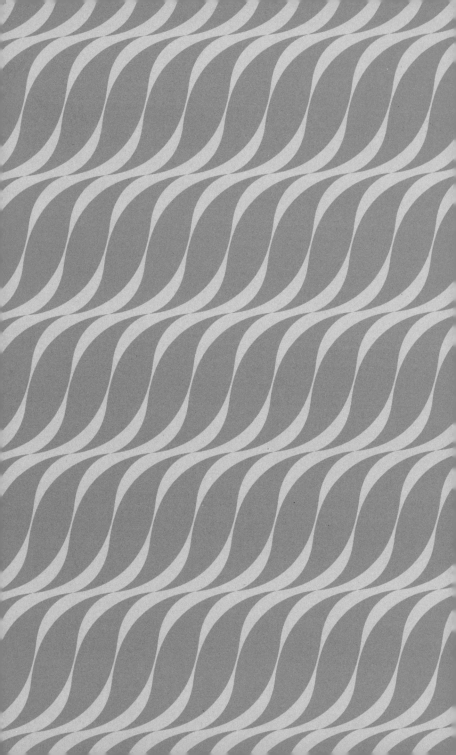